The Manager's Pocket Guide to Performance Management

Sharon G. Fisher

HRD Press
Amherst, Massachusetts

D1002800

Published by: **HRD Press, Inc.**
                  22 Amherst Road
                  Amherst, MA 01002
                  (800) 822-2801
                  (413) 253-3490 (fax)
                  www.hrdpress.com

ISBN 0-87425-419-1

Production and design by Jean Miller
Cover design by Eileen Klockars
Editorial services by Robie Grant

Introduction

The purpose of this pocket guide is to provide managers with practical tools for enhancing employee performance. The guide includes the following information:

Overview: Identifying Employee Development Needs

Overview: Identifying Employee Development Needs

Competency and productivity are essential for organizational success in the 21st century. A key ingredient for such success is human capital, and investing in our human capital will be critical for organizational survival.

This is a globally competitive environment, marked by high velocity change. Successful businesses keep up by getting ahead of that change; they get ahead by growing and learning; and they grow and learn by investing in their workforce.

Throughout the world, organizations that are at the forefront of effectiveness and competitiveness constantly seek to:

- Improve the productivity of their people

- Identify their needs in terms of the gap between desired or required performance levels and current performance

- Select the appropriate strategies for enhancing employee performance, focusing on results and continuous improvement, and motivating their workforce to higher levels of quality

- Integrate human resources functions with new technology and capabilities

- Evaluate the outcomes of performance enhancement strategies to determine if further analysis is required.

Although training, development, and other human resource services are critical to increasing competence, meeting the educational challenge is just part of the answer. An effective system must focus on the broader issues of improving performance by integrating human resource solutions with organizational needs and priorities.

When identifying employee training and development needs, it is important to use systems thinking. Systems thinking recognizes that everything is interrelated, and that an action or event in one part of the whole affects all of the other parts. A systems thinking perspective will ensure that individual employee development is aligned to an organization's mission, corporate goals, and operational requirements. Systematically planned training and development will help an organization be successful in its mission. Successful training and development programs depend on systematic application of the process. Once the benefits of successful training are felt and shared by the organization and its employees, enthusiasm toward the process of learning and development can help to create a learning organization.

Let's take a look at how a systems thinking approach can work within an organization.

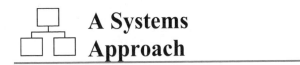

A Systems Approach

The diagram below illustrates a systems approach to identifying and evaluating employee development needs and performance enhancement strategies.

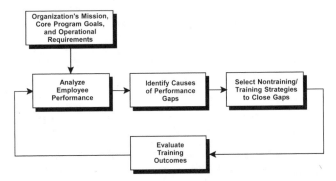

This systematic approach to training and development will ensure that workers do not undertake training for the sake of training (training for activity), but rather engage in worthwhile and useful training (training for impact). The following paragraphs present an overview of each phase of the process.

Mission, Core Program Goals, and Operational Requirements

Initially, an organization's mission, core program goals, and operational requirements are reviewed to identify overall performance requirements and current agency-wide training priorities. The following describes the process of relating mission requirements to training in greater detail.

ANALYZING EMPLOYEE PERFORMANCE

The next phase is to establish desired employee performance levels by examining expectations (based on an organization's mission) and identifying performance indicators for your organization. Once you have a clear picture of desired or required performance levels, the next step is to analyze current performance to determine if there is a performance gap between desired performance and actual performance that needs to be addressed.

IDENTIFYING CAUSES OF PERFORMANCE GAPS

If you determine that such a gap exists, you must then explore reasons why the performance gap exists. This step is critically important. For example, if the performance gap is related to organizational or motivational factors rather than a lack of knowledge or skills, training dollars should not be invested in trying to solve the performance problem.

SELECTING NONTRAINING/TRAINING STRATEGIES TO CLOSE GAPS

Once you have determined the cause of any performance gaps, you must select appropriate strategies to address the performance problem(s). Training and development may **not** be the appropriate solution for a performance problem. With some performance problems, nontraining strategies would work best. Training should only be used when you have systematically determined that it will address the performance problem.

EVALUATING TRAINING OUTCOMES

The next phase in the process is to evaluate the outcomes of your strategies to determine if they have resolved the performance gap. The process doesn't stop here; information from your evaluation is then fed back into future needs assessments.

Answers to questions such as "Did the training work?" and "Was the investment in training worth it?" will help you monitor the effectiveness of training and development strategies and make effective decisions about future training investments.

Relating Mission Requirements to Training

A systems approach to training and development provides a method to link individual training to the strategic and operational goals of the organization. Linking learning to the strategic goals is critical to the success of a knowledge-based, service-focused organization.

DETERMINING OVERALL TRAINING PRIORITIES

Each year, you should re-examine your organizational training priorities. You can use the process shown below to assess needs:

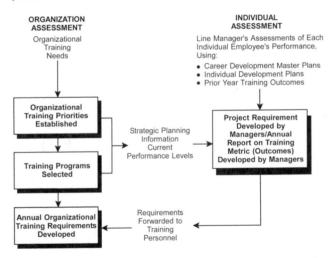

During the training needs assessment process, information is gathered from a variety of sources, including strategic planning, organizational performance indicators, and interviews with managers.

As a manager, your role in the process is to develop an annual training plan based on individual employee training needs. In addition, you are responsible for evaluating the results of training to make sure the training is achieving the desired results. This process ensures that cost-effective and appropriate developmental opportunities are aligned with organizational goals and objectives.

GATHERING ORGANIZATIONAL INFORMATION

It is important that you have current information on the organization's mission, core business, and operational requirements in order to link them to the performance of your work units. To create and maintain a shared vision, you must ensure that your employees always have the most current information possible, and you must continually develop their ability to understand how their own work supports the organization's overall direction.

Summary

You have just reviewed the basic principles behind employee development. Once you have determined the overall training priorities and have gathered and reviewed pertinent information, you are ready to begin the employee development process. This process is described in the sections that follow.

Fostering a Learning Organization

- Learning Organization Overview
- The Learning Organization

Analyzing Employee Performance

- Establish Desired Performance Levels
- Determine Current Performance Levels
- Identify Performance Gaps

Identifying Causes of Performance Gaps

- Determine the Extent of the Problem
- Pinpoint the Reasons for the Gap

Nontraining and Training Strategies for Enhancing Performance

- Select Nontraining Strategies
- Select Training Strategies

Managing Training Resources

- Weigh Costs and Benefits
- Acquire Training Resources

Promoting Training Transfer

Promoting Training Transfer...
- Before Training
- During Training
- After Training

Evaluating Training Outcomes

- Determine the Value of Training
- Make Continuous Improvements

Fostering a Learning Organization

Some organizations conduct business with an *"if it isn't broken, don't fix it"* attitude, until the day they learn that they have to make major changes in their organization if they are to continue to compete.

A learning organization is one that continually expands its ability to shape its future. For a modern knowledge-based, service-focused business to survive and be successful, learning must be linked to the strategic goals of the organization. The organization's goal is to make continual learning a way of organizational life in order to improve the performance of the organization as a total system.

The Learning Organization: An Overview

According to Peter Senge, a leading expert in the field of organizational management, the core of learning organization work is based upon five learning disciplines or continuous programs of study and practice. These "learning disciplines" are shown in the illustration below.

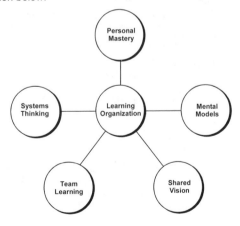

Personal Mastery. Personal mastery is learning to expand personal capacity to create desired results. It also means creating an organizational environment that encourages all its members to develop themselves. You, as a manager, cannot increase someone else's personal mastery, but you can set up conditions that encourage and support people who want to increase their own.

It is important to offer employees encouragement and support because learning does not occur in any enduring way unless it is sparked by a person's own ardent interest and curiosity. Without that spark, an individual might still accept training in a subject, and the effects will last for a while. Without commitment, trainees may stop learning the new skills. If, however, learning is related to a person's own vision, then that person will do whatever he or she can to keep learning alive.

Mental Models. Mental models are the images, assumptions, and experiences that people carry in their minds about themselves, other people, institutions, and the organization. Mental models determine what people see and shape how they act. This learning discipline involves reflecting upon, clarifying, and improving your internal assumptions about the organization, and seeing how these assumptions shape your actions and decisions.

When people are unaware of or unwilling to change their mental models, then learning may be very limited. The core task of this discipline is to bring mental models to the surface, to explore and talk about them with minimal defensiveness, and to find ways to create new mental models that serve the organization better and facilitate learning. Truly understanding others' points of view and learning from each other requires us to develop and practice skills in reflection (becoming more aware of how we form our mental models) and inquiry (openly sharing views and developing knowledge about each other's assumptions).

Shared Vision. Building a sense of commitment among people means first developing a shared image of the future, and then identifying the principles and guiding practices to get there. Managers must be visibly willing to take a stand for the guiding ideas they consider important, while remaining open to involvement and points of view from others.

At the heart of this discipline is creating a sense of purpose that binds people together and propels them to fulfill their deepest aspirations. Building shared vision is an ongoing process in which all team members articulate shared understandings of vision, purpose, values, why their work matters, and how it fits into the larger world.

Team Learning. Team learning is promoting team skill development so that the team's ability is greater than the sum of the individuals' talents. Poor communication between people and between organizations can be a major block to learning and continuous improvement. Team learning is about enhancing a team's capacity to think and act in new synergistic ways, with full coordination and a sense of unity.

Team learning means teams need to work together to think insightfully about complex issues, to act in ways that complement each other's actions, and to continually foster other learning teams by instilling practices and skills of team learning throughout the organization.

The discipline of team learning is centered on mastering team communication. Teams should be able to freely and creatively explore complex and subtle issues by listening to each other and suspending personal views. Team members should be able to present and defend different views as they search for the best view to support decisions that must be made. And team learning means learning how to deal creatively with the forces that oppose productive dialogue and discussion in working teams.

Systems Thinking. Systems thinking is a way of thinking that focuses on the interrelationships within systems. Systems thinking recognizes that everything is interrelated, and that an action or event in one part of the whole affects all of the other parts. In systems thinking, the structure of an organization includes the traditional hierarchy and process flows, but it also includes attitudes and perceptions, the quality of products and customer services, and many other factors.

Systems thinking recognizes that changes intended to improve performance in one part of the organization can affect other parts of the organization with surprising and often negative consequences. For example, decisions based solely on information at the local level can be counterproductive to the system as a whole. Systems thinking also involves learning to develop processes that integrate people horizontally and across functions.

 For further information on learning organizations and the core learning disciplines, see *The Fifth Discipline: The Art and Practice of the Learning Organization,* by Peter M. Senge (1990) and *The Fifth Discipline Fieldbook,* by Peter Senge and other authors (1994).

Managers and the Learning Organization

Everyone in an organization contributes to the organization's culture. The people who contribute most to an enterprise are the people who are committed to practicing these learning disciplines themselves—expanding their own capacity to hold and seek a vision, to reflect and inquire, to build collective capabilities, and to understand systems.

In learning organizations, you, as a manager, have a particular responsibility. Your performance, conversations, and actions demonstrate what values you believe are important to the organization. A learning organization cannot exist without its managers' commitment and leadership. You must demonstrate belief in the organization and the people who are members of it. The core competencies or learning disciplines are the vehicle for growing and developing this kind of leadership.

A growing number of organizations are transforming themselves into learning organizations. The following paragraphs describe how you can develop the components.

PERSONAL MASTERY

In the past, education ended when an individual received credentials. Now, education is considered continuous, deliberate organizational learning. A comprehensive career management system (CMS) can be developed that will provide systematic career progression and training for personnel in each stage of their careers. To create this system, competencies necessary for many critical organizational areas are identified and ways to assess current skill levels are researched. In addition, a continuing education program is created that will identify important continuing education topics and training needs for the workforce. The CMS will enhance an organizational environment that encourages all members to continually develop themselves.

MENTAL MODELS

The stability and security traditionally associated with corporate jobs are being replaced by accelerated change, speed, and a reinvented, entrepreneurial system that requires the workforce to remain competitive and marketable. These changes have a significant impact on the organization's ability to gain and sustain a well-trained workforce with leading-edge technical skills and managerial abilities. In a more competitive and uncertain environment, organizations must have workforces with the skills and flexibility to successfully meet their missions wherever and whenever the need arises.

To empower a responsive, flexible workforce, traditional ways of doing business must be re-evaluated. Performance support systems and new approaches to job placement can be developed. Also, a job rotational system can be designed to support the development of a multi-skilled workforce. Finally, the organization should create an assessment system that identifies employees with high potential for multitasking.

SHARED VISION

The organization's top management must be devoted to building a sense of commitment among personnel by developing a shared vision of the organization's future. This may be accomplished by holding "all-hands" meetings and distributing materials that establish a shared understanding of the organization's mission and vision and the values of all employees.

TEAM LEARNING

Individual assignments and hierarchical taskings will give way in the learning organization to high-performance work teams that own and manage business processes. Guidelines for matrix management can be developed to include an information system and management structure to support management in quickly identifying, bringing together, and tasking a team of employees to do a job.

SYSTEMS THINKING

Employees must be empowered and encouraged to form partnerships to maximize their exposure to various issues. The workforce that was once stove-piped and single-focused will need to be diversified, fully networked, and knowledgeable across organizational functions in the learning organization. This process can be facilitated through informational formal and informal networking (holding monthly brown bag luncheons with colleagues, for example).

Learning Organization
Managerial Self-Assessment

Instructions:

Use the self-assessment on the following pages to determine the extent to which you, your team(s), and your own organization are moving toward becoming a learning organization.

- Read each statement.

- Indicate the degree to which you believe the item accurately describes your own behavior by checking the appropriate box:

SA	=	Strongly Agree
A	=	Agree
D	=	Disagree
SD	=	Strongly Disagree

- Follow the directions for scoring the self-assessment on page 24.

- Interpret your score using the scale on page 25.

*   *   *

Learning Organization
Managerial Self-Assessment

	SA	A	D	SD
1. Each individual I supervise feels he or she is doing something that matters—personally and to the larger world.	❏	❏	❏	❏
2. I find ways to ensure that my employees are stretching, growing, and enhancing their capacities.	❏	❏	❏	❏
3. When I want something really creative done, I ask a team to do it instead of sending one person off to do it alone.	❏	❏	❏	❏
4. I reward and recognize honesty and openness in the people I supervise.	❏	❏	❏	❏
5. I promote and reward partnering at all levels of our organization, particularly across functions.	❏	❏	❏	❏
6. I share credit for our work unit's successes with all the members of my team.	❏	❏	❏	❏
7. I encourage discussion among my employees about our vision and where our organization fits within that vision.	❏	❏	❏	❏
8. I share relevant information with all the people I supervise, even if this involves educating them to understand that information.	❏	❏	❏	❏
9. I make it possible for my employees to learn what is going on at every level of the organization so they can understand how their actions influence others.	❏	❏	❏	❏

	SA	A	D	SD
10. The people I supervise feel free to inquire about and address each other's assumptions and biases.	❑	❑	❑	❑
11. My employees feel that they are able to openly discuss any work-related item with me and with other team members.	❑	❑	❑	❑
12. My employees and I treat each other as valued colleagues.	❑	❑	❑	❑
13. The people I supervise demonstrate a mutual respect and trust in the way they talk to each other and work together, regardless of what positions they hold.	❑	❑	❑	❑
14. My employees feel free to experiment, take risks, and openly assess the results.	❑	❑	❑	❑
15. I am personally involved in structured team discussion sessions to demonstrate that the team of people I supervise is important to me.	❑	❑	❑	❑
16. I try to ensure that there is always a consistent "critical mass" of committed people on any team so that the work of the team can always move forward.	❑	❑	❑	❑
17. I strive to create and maintain an atmosphere of trust for team discussion sessions.	❑	❑	❑	❑
18. I raise questions with no hard and firm answers to show my employees that I want to learn from what they have to say and that I don't always know the answers.	❑	❑	❑	❑

Determining Your Overall Score

		SA	A	D	SD
1.	Beginning on page 22, total the check-marks for each category.				
2.	Multiply the number of checkmarks you entered on line 1 by…	**4**	**3**	**2**	**1**
3.	Enter the result of line 1 multiplied by line 2.				

4. Total the four scores in line 3.

INTERPRETING THE LEARNING ORGANIZATION:
MANAGERIAL SELF-ASSESSMENT

The purpose of this self-assessment is to help you assess the extent to which you have been able to foster and manage a learning organization for your employees. Use the table below to interpret your score.

Self-Assessment Score Interpretation Table

OVERALL SCORE	INTERPRETATION
1 to 18	You need to expand your fundamental knowledge of the learning disciplines and characteristics of a learning organization.
19 to 36	You are already exhibiting some characteristics of fostering a learning organization but need to improve your skills.
37 to 54	You are well on the way to fostering and managing a learning organization environment for your employees.
Over 54	You already exhibit the characteristics of a manager who has created a learning organization atmosphere for your own employees.

Tools for Creating a Learning Organization

To create a learning organization, you have to create opportunities for people to share experiences and learn from each other. New knowledge has to be immediately transformed into action as an integral part of employee training. You will need to employ a variety of strategies and tools to create this kind of learning environment for your people. When used wisely and appropriately, training and development is an important management tool.

The remainder of the sections in this book describe employee development strategies and the tools available to managers. You are now ready to proceed to the first phase of employee development, ***Analyzing Employee Performance.***

Analyzing Employee Performance

Managers have to know how to deal with employees who do not perform up to standards. The purpose of this section is to provide information on how to analyze employee performance and identify any gaps between desired and actual performance.

Performance analysis is the first step: identify current or future performance requirements; determine if current performance levels meet the identified requirements; and identify any gaps between desired and actual performance. The gap between desired and actual performance might be a *potential* training need.

Performance Analysis: Three Steps

The basic objective of performance analysis is to close the gap between optimum work performance levels and actual work performance. To analyze performance, follow these steps:

Step 1: Establish desired performance levels.

- Identify expectations.
- Review performance indicators.

Step 2: Determine current performance levels.

- Select measurement techniques.
- Collect data.

Step 3: Identify performance gaps.

- Analyze the data.
- Calculate the performance gap.

Each of the steps used to analyze performance is explained on the following pages.

Step 1: Establish Desired Performance Levels.

The first step in establishing desired levels of employee performance is to determine how employees *should* be performing, according to expectations held by the organization's customers (or stakeholders) and according to established organizational performance standards.

To establish desired performance levels, you must first identify the expectations of your customers, and then review performance indicators for each position in your work unit. Let's begin the process of analyzing employee performance by identifying expectations.

IDENTIFY EXPECTATIONS.

The expectations of your internal and external customers should influence how your employees perform. Each manager/work unit should know the expectations of its internal and external customers. If you have not identified your customers' expectations, you may want to:

1. **List all key stakeholders:** People who:
   - Can influence resources or inputs used by your work unit
   - Are affected by services or outputs being provided
   - Have an interest in expected outcomes of your work unit

2. **Next, determine stakeholder needs and expectations.** For each stakeholder, state what this individual or group of individuals needs and/or expects from your work unit. These statements should be very specific, and should come directly from the stakeholder, whenever possible. (See the example on the next page).

STAKEHOLDER	EXPECTATIONS
Acme Computer Chip Company	➤ Services/products will be delivered by agreed-upon date.
	➤ Inquiries will be answered within 48 hours.
	➤ Services/products will meet all specifications.
	➤ All work will be within agreed-upon budget.

Wherever possible, interview or survey your customers to elicit feedback on whether their needs and requirements are being met. Collecting feedback will help you stay focused on critical performance indicators.

REVIEW PERFORMANCE INDICATORS.

Once you have identified your stakeholder expectations, you can establish performance indicators. Before establishing new performance indicators, you should determine if performance indicators have been established for each position in your work unit.

If so... Make sure that the indicators are consistent with the stakeholder expectations.

If not... Establish performance indicators. Performance indicators include the following components:

Noun Phrase: A description of what is being measured.

Unit of Measure: Number, percentage, or level of the desired performance.

Adjective Clarifier: A further description of what is being measured.

For example:

UNIT OF MEASURE	NOUN PHRASE	ADJECTIVE CLARIFIER
Percentage of	products passing quality inspections	conducted by Quality Control Inspector
Number of	errors in data entry	within each batch of computer chips
Amount of	time to fix communication problems	within 5 minutes of notification
Level of	customer satisfaction ratings	measured by customer survey conducted 60 days after services are provided

Make sure that you use all existing data on required performance levels when establishing performance indicators. Also, double-check that the performance indicators you establish are consistent with your stakeholders' expectations and with the overall mission requirements of your organization.

You are now ready for the next step in the process, *Determine Current Performance Levels.*

Step 2: Determine Current Performance Levels.

After you have identified the desired performance levels, the next step is to develop a clear picture of what is actually happening now. You need to consider:

- How are people presently performing?
- What results are now being achieved?

To answer these questions, you must first select a technique by which to measure current employee performance, and then begin collecting data.

SELECT MEASUREMENT TECHNIQUES.

There are many different tools that you can use to measure current performance. This section reviews the following types of performance measurement tools: *run charts, Pareto charts,* and *flowcharts.*

Note: You may want to use multiple tools to help you identify and analyze performance problems. For example, you may be able to monitor outputs using a run chart and only use a Pareto chart if a problem is identified.

Run Charts

Description: A run chart helps you track some aspect of process performance over time (e.g., error rates, outputs, response time, complaints, etc.). A run chart gives you visual clues about how a process is operating, and whether it is improving, deteriorating, or staying the same over time.

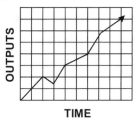

Uses: Use a run chart when you want to:

✓ Identify performance trends

✓ Compare two similar processes (such as between two work units)

✓ Compare the same work unit over two different time periods

Tips:

➢ Choose the right variable or element (e.g., output volume, cycle/down time, new work, etc.) to measure so that it accurately reflects what is happening in the process.

➢ Chart only the things you believe matter most to the quality and productivity of an important process.

➢ Make sure the data are plotted in a time-ordered sequence.

➢ Plot time or sequence on the horizontal axis and the variable being counted or measured on the vertical axis.

➢ Update the chart frequently.

➢ Make the data gathering as easy as possible and have the people involved in the process gather the data and update the charts.

➢ Always show what is being measured, when it was measured, and anything else that will help the chart reader understand what is happening.

Pareto Charts

Description: A Pareto chart is a simple bar graph that ranks the causes, sources, types, or reasons for performance problems in order of importance. A Pareto chart helps you determine what to work on to get the greatest improvements.

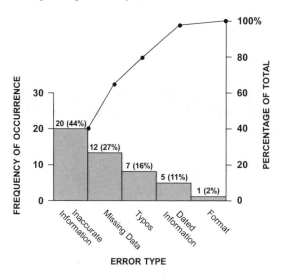

Uses: Use a Pareto chart when:

✓ The performance area being analyzed is complex

✓ There is a large amount of data and you need to separate out the "vital few" items to work on

✓ You want to prioritize and select solutions

Tips:

➤ Before constructing a Pareto chart, it is important that you organize the problems or causes into a small number of categories to analyze. The Pareto chart is most effective when you are analyzing eight or fewer items.

➤ Select a standard unit of measurement (e.g., errors, defects, frequency, size, etc.) and the time period to be analyzed. When selecting the time period, allow enough time to gather the required information.

➤ Use a worksheet to summarize the data.

ERROR TYPE	TOTAL OCCURRENCE	PERCENTAGE OF TOTAL ERRORS
Inaccurate Information	20	44
Missing Data	12	27
Typographical Errors	7	16
Dated Information	5	11
Format	1	2
TOTALS	**45**	**100**

➤ Plot the data by arranging the bars in descending order.

➤ Analyze the data by breaking down the causes further and further until the solution becomes obvious. If necessary, make a subchart of each one to understand the problem better.

➤ Identify the items that account for the highest percentage of the problem and work on those.

Flowcharts

Description: A flowchart is a map showing how the work process is accomplished. A flowchart shows a systematic sequence of steps to take in completing a job. A flowchart "language" is used to classify the activities using the following symbols:

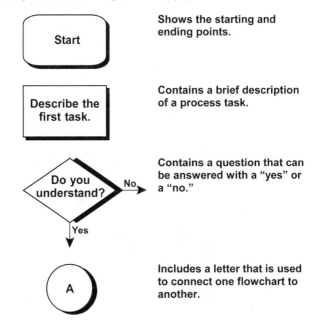

Shows the starting and ending points.

Contains a brief description of a process task.

Contains a question that can be answered with a "yes" or a "no."

Includes a letter that is used to connect one flowchart to another.

Uses: Use a flowchart when you need to:

✓ Document or describe an existing process

✓ Investigate where problems might occur in a process

✓ Identify specific areas for improvement (e.g., rework loops, delays, multiple inspections or authorizations, etc.)

✓ Design and/or standardize an entirely new process

✓ Identify how, when, or where to measure an existing process to see if it complies with requirements

✓ Analyze how time is used

✓ Identify customers, suppliers, or other impacted people

Tips:

➢ Decide early on where the process to be studied will start and end, what operations will be included, and how much detail will be appropriate.

➢ Define the first and last steps. Then document the remaining steps in sequence.

➢ Make sure the "right" people help construct the chart. The people doing the work should chart the process.

➢ Start with a simple chart and add detail as needed.

➢ Gather additional data by observing the process and/or talking to the people involved.

➢ Have people other than those who designed the chart read through it to check for accuracy and completeness.

COLLECT DATA.

After you have selected your measurement technique, you are ready to begin collecting data. Collecting data does not have to be a labor-intensive, time-consuming process. It is usually not necessary to collect huge amounts of information, but it is true that collecting some data is always better than having no data at all.

Data can be quickly collected through the use of standardized forms such as checksheets and surveys and it can come from previously generated reports. You can use a spreadsheet program to input data and generate reports.

Tips:

➤ Find and use existing information whenever possible. You may have all the information you need in your files.

➤ Collect only information that you plan to use. Make sure you know how you intend to use any piece of data before you go to the effort of collecting it.

➤ Concentrate your efforts on the most important information sources. If you can only collect a small amount of information, make sure you include information from the most critical sources.

➤ Use the simplest data collection techniques that will work. Use ready-made instruments and modify them to meet your needs.

➤ Collect data from more than one source to strengthen and confirm your findings and make them more credible.

➤ Use computer programs to organize and classify information as you collect it.

You are now ready for the third step, ***Identify Performance Gaps.***

Step 3: Identify Performance Gaps.

The next step in the process is to determine if there are gaps between how people are currently performing and how they should be performing. If your analysis of the performance data indicates that there is a performance gap, you will have to determine the extent of the gap and, correspondingly, how best to address it.

To identify performance gaps, you must begin by analyzing the data. Then calculate the gaps in performance.

ANALYZE THE DATA.

After you have collected the data, you should first check the quality of the data for accuracy and completeness.

1. **Check the data.** To check the quality of the data, give the data an overall "eyeball" appraisal and ask the following questions:

   - Is the performance data accurate, complete, and current?
   - Are the data and reported events close to your expectations?
   - Are there any unexpected differences from any data collected earlier?

2. **Confirm the data.** If you find discrepancies among the data, or if you want to confirm the data, you should:

   - Check the collected data against another source (e.g., work samples, error reports, complaint records, supervisor feedback, etc.).
   - Collect another sample of the same data so that you can determine the degree of accuracy and reliability of the original performance data collected.
   - Review any similar information that may exist about the job (e.g., job descriptions).

3. **Summarize the data.** Once you have validated the data you collected, you are ready to organize and tabulate it. Quantitative data can be summarized using simple descriptive statistics (e.g., averages, distributions, etc.) found in spreadsheet programs. Qualitative data (not numeric) should be presented using an approach logic such as by chronological progression of steps, cause-and-effect, grouping similar items (e.g., job tasks, job outputs), etc.

CALCULATE THE PERFORMANCE GAP.

The final activity in analyzing performance is to calculate the performance gap. Calculating the gap is a simple process of comparing the desired performance levels identified in Step 1 with actual performance levels determined in Step 2.

   VERSUS

Desired   **Actual**

Once you have determined that there is a gap between the desired and actual performance levels, answer the following questions about the gap:

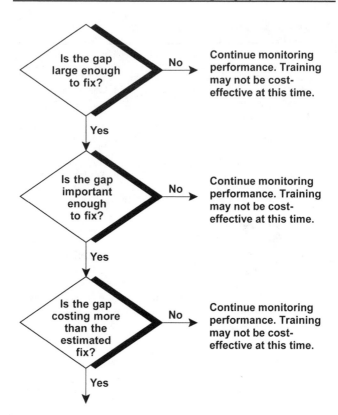

You may now proceed to the next phase: *Identifying Causes of Performance Gaps.*

Summary

You have just learned the steps for analyzing employee performance. The next section in this book will be *Identifying Causes of Performance Gaps.* To learn more about analyzing employee performance, refer to the following publications:

Gilbert, T. (1978). *Human competence: Engineering worthy performance.* New York: McGraw-Hill.

Harless, J. H. (1970). *An ounce of analysis.* Falls Church, Virginia: Harless Educational Technologists, Inc.

Mager, R. F. and Pipe, P. (1970). *Analyzing performance problems.* Belmont, California: Fearon.

Identifying Causes of Performance Gaps

After you have collected and analyzed performance data and concluded that there is a performance gap, the next step is to determine the most likely causes of the gap.

It is important to determine the *causes* of performance gaps because solutions fail if they are selected to treat only visible symptoms, rather than the underlying causes. When you identify root causes of a problem, you are much more likely to significantly reduce or eliminate the problem.

Once you have identified why the performance gap exists, you will be able to determine whether nontraining or training strategies for closing the gap are appropriate.

Gap Analysis: Two Steps

To identify the causes of performance gaps, follow these steps:

Step 1: Determine the extent of the problem.
- Identify the magnitude.
- Identify trends.

Step 2: Pinpoint the reasons for the gap.
- Identify possible reasons for gaps.
- Select most likely reasons.

The following pages explain each of the steps used to identify the causes of performance gaps.

Step 1: Determine the Extent of the Problem.

The first step in identifying causes of performance gaps is to determine the extent and degree of the performance gap.

IDENTIFY THE MAGNITUDE.

As you interpret the data, ask yourself questions such as:

✓ How many people exhibit this performance gap?

✓ Is the gap limited to specific occupational areas?

✓ Are some office locations affected more than others?

IDENTIFY TRENDS.

Try to identify trends in the data, such as patterns of high and low performance. Ask questions such as:

✓ Is the gap increasing or decreasing over time?

✓ Do high and low performers tend to be in certain groups or regions, or are they distributed equally throughout the organization?

✓ Is the gap as common among both experienced and inexperienced personnel?

✓ Is the gap constant over time, or is it triggered by some event?

✓ Are there performance differences among units, regions, or departments?

✓ Are there differences among employees previously trained by one method or school or another?

Continue to determine the extent of the problem until you have a complete picture of the performance gap.

Step 2: Pinpoint the Reasons for the Gap.

Next, you should try to determine the cause or source of the gap as accurately as possible, because some performance gaps are best addressed by training and some are not.

IDENTIFY POSSIBLE REASONS FOR GAPS.

There are three kinds of factors that can influence people's performance:

- ✓ Environmental factors
- ✓ Motivational factors
- ✓ Knowledge/skill factors

Use the next three charts to review these factors.

ENVIRONMENTAL FACTORS	
Symptoms	**Determine whether or not...**
The employees know how to perform, are motivated to perform, but still are not performing as expected.	Employees have inadequate tools, resources, or information.
	Employees are interrupted frequently.
Prescription	Job standards are *not* communicated explicitly and in a timely fashion.
Determine if the employees could perform as required if the conditions were changed. If so, change the environmental factor(s) influencing performance. It is unlikely that training will solve the problem.	Employees have complained about working conditions.
	Rules make task completion more difficult.
	No standard operating procedures exist.
	Many employees have the same problems.

ENVIRONMENTAL FACTORS

Symptoms

If the employees *could* perform adequately if they had to, but do not, then a lack of motivation or flawed incentives may be influencing their performance.

Prescription

If motivation is the problem, add positive incentives and remove disincentives. It is unlikely that training alone will solve the problem.

Determine whether or not...

The employees could perform the task as required if their lives depended on it.

There is anything about the task that frustrates the employees.

The employees receive praise for adequate performance.

There are any negative consequences of adequate performance.

There are advantages to the employees for poor performance.

The employees are informed about the quality of their performance.

KNOWLEDGE/SKILL FACTORS

Symptoms

If employees are motivated to perform as expected and the job environment is not negatively influencing performance, then the employees may not know *how* to perform as expected.

Prescription

Lack of knowledge/skills can be solved through training.

Determine whether or not...

Employees have ever performed the task adequately.

Employees have received specific training for the task.

The task is performed infrequently.

Employees always perform the task incorrectly.

SELECT MOST-LIKELY REASONS.

To select the most likely reason for the performance gap, you should review the trends or patterns in the data that you have collected. Listed below are some patterns that are commonly found:

For gaps likely due to lack of knowledge, skills, attitudes, and/or practice:

✓ Performance tends to improve with time.

✓ High and low performers tend to be distributed throughout the entire organization.

✓ People cannot perform as desired, even if their lives depended on it.

For gaps likely due to environmental or motivational factors:

✓ Employee performance levels off or declines over time.

✓ High and low performers tend to be only in certain groups or areas.

✓ Tasks are not being performed to standards.

✓ Employees do not believe there is reason for them to perform as desired.

✓ Deadlines are not being met.

✓ There is a work backlog.

✓ Employees are performing up to individual performance standards, but the overall quality of work does not match customer needs or the organization's mission requirements.

✓ Employees perform as desired only when actually observed.

✓ You have reason to believe employees are "under-achievers."

Tips:

➢ Involve employees when identifying and selecting reasons for performance gaps.

➢ Explore all possibilities before narrowing. Use brainstorming techniques to identify all possible reasons before selecting the causes. One effective brainstorming technique is to have employees identify all reasons and write those reasons on sticky notes (one per note). Group the sticky notes into categories and label each category.

➢ Develop a diagram that shows the relationships between causes and effects. A fishbone chart can be used to show causes and effects. A fishbone chart is structured as follows:

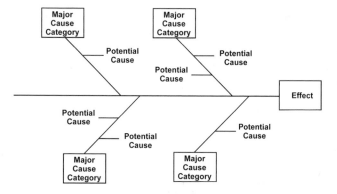

➢ Identify the effect (problem, process, condition) and write the effect in the box on the right side of the diagram.

➢ Identify the major cause categories and enter these in the boxes diagonal to the main horizontal line.

➤ Brainstorm potential causes of the problem, decide under which major cause category they should be placed, and write them on the horizontal lines under each major cause category.

➤ Review the potential causes and look for causes that appear in more than one major cause category. This is an indication of a *most likely cause*. Circle the most likely causes.

➤ Review the most likely causes and ask *Why is this a cause?* Write your answers on a separate piece of paper or on a flipchart.

➤ After narrowing down the most likely causes, choose from that group what you believe are the *most probable causes*.

➤ Wrap up the session by making assignments to gather data to prove or disprove the most probable causes.

Summary

You have just learned how to determine the extent of any performance problems among your employees and how to identify why the problems occurred. The next phase is to select strategies for improving or enhancing employee performance. These strategies are described in the next section, **Selecting Nontraining and Training Strategies.**

Selecting Nontraining
and Training Strategies

Y ou now know that you have a performance gap that is worth addressing. You also have identified the likely causes of the performance gap. The following pages describe the various strategies you can use for selecting either a nontraining or training method for closing the performance gaps.

Selecting Nontraining and Training Strategies

There are two types of strategies for enhancing employee performance: **nontraining** strategies and **training** strategies.

It is important to match the type of strategy used to the causes of the gap in performance.

- If your causes are due to environmental or motivational factors, then you should review the section on **selecting nontraining strategies.**

- If your causes are due to skill/knowledge deficiencies, then you should review the section on **selecting training strategies.**

Selecting Nontraining Strategies

Nontraining strategies should be chosen when performance gaps are caused by deficiencies in the environment, flawed incentives, or lack of motivation. Here are some of the most common nontraining strategies:

- Change feedback methods.
- Modify reward systems.
- Improve employee selection practices.
- Redesign the organization.

Let's take a look at how each of these nontraining strategies can impact employee performance.

CHANGE FEEDBACK METHODS.

Description: Changing feedback methods involves changing the quantity, quality, and/or timeliness of feedback that you give your employees about what they do, how well they do it, what results they achieve, or how well their work results match up to desired results.

Uses: You should consider changing feedback methods:

✓ When the performance gap is due to motivational factors

✓ When the employee has been able to perform at the required level in the past

✓ After training, to reinforce new skills and knowledge

Tips:

➢ Use coaching on a short-term basis to provide timely, immediate, and concrete feedback.

➢ Display production wall charts that give immediate, concrete feedback to employees about how much or how well individuals or work groups are performing.

➢ Use written feedback to provide short, practical, how-to-do-it guidance on handling common or unique problem situations.

➢ Use information from internal or external customer surveys to communicate how well employees are meeting the needs and requirements of customers.

➢ Use peer assessment to build team communication and feedback.

MODIFY REWARD SYSTEMS.

Description: A reward system is the organization's way of linking employee actions to positive consequences. A reward system attracts people to join the organization, keeps them working, and motivates them to perform. There are many theories about human motivation and reward, but basically all conclude that employees generally do what they are rewarded for doing, avoid what they are punished for doing, and neglect what they are neither punished nor rewarded for doing. To perform successfully, employees must feel they can succeed and they must be able to count on receiving a reward they value.

Uses: You should consider modifying your reward system when:

✓ Employees expect that no reward will result from desired performance

✓ Rewards for performing are of no value to the employee

✓ Employees perceive the rewards for performing as negative

✓ Individual incentives discourage team performance

Tips:

➤ Design incentives to deliberately encourage performance that meets job performance or organizational goals.

➤ Be creative in designing nonmonetary rewards such as choice of projects or job enrichment.

➤ Look for opportunities to reward team as well as individual performance.

IMPROVE EMPLOYEE SELECTION PRACTICES.

Description: Improving employee selection practices means making sure that you match people to jobs or assignments for which they are qualified or suited. Selection methods influence training because the knowledge, skills, and attitudes that people bring to the job influence what they must learn in order to perform as desired.

Uses: You should consider improving your employee selection systems when:

- ✓ Turnover is high

- ✓ Employees are complaining that their work activities are different from what they were expecting

- ✓ Supervisors and managers are complaining that their employees are ill-equipped to perform, even after training

Tips:

- ➢ Make sure that job descriptions describe what your people are responsible for doing and the results they are expected to achieve.

- ➢ Develop job descriptions that are complete, accurate, and current.

- ➢ Use highly structured employment interview guides to aid in your selection process.

- ➢ Consult with personnel specialists to ensure that you are following selection guidelines.

- ➢ Get training in interviewing and selection techniques.

REDESIGN THE ORGANIZATION.

Description: Organizational redesign is the process of changing assigned objectives, responsibilities, or reporting relationships within an organization. This can include any change in the contents, methods, and relationships of jobs to meet individual or organizational requirements.

Uses: You should consider redesigning your organization when:

✓ Employees are confused about job responsibilities

✓ Job descriptions are vague or unclear

✓ Organizational charts do not reflect actual organizational relationships

✓ Your organizational structure fails to relate to the organization's strategic goals

✓ There are pockets of employees doing too much or too little work, or doing boring work

✓ Workflow processes result in unnecessary complexity, inefficiency, or wasted resources

✓ You cannot adapt quickly enough to changing internal or external conditions (e.g., new customers or unusual requests from customers)

Tips:

➢ Describe explicitly what people should do, how they should do it, and what results are desirable in line with the organization's goals and objectives.

➢ If you change reporting relationships, be careful not to create an unnecessary management layer through which approvals must pass.

➢ Improve information-sharing by analyzing what, how much, when, and how information is communicated.

➢ Involve your employees in the redesign effort. If your employees are represented by a union, make sure that changes in working conditions are negotiated.

Selecting Training Strategies

There are many ways to provide training. In a learning organization, training often occurs through work-based learning opportunities, which are alternatives to traditional classroom training courses. The following pages provide an overview of both traditional training and alternative learning methods.

Training Methods

First you must decide the type of training methods to be used. The flowchart on the following page lists the questions you should ask when deciding if classroom-based training is appropriate.

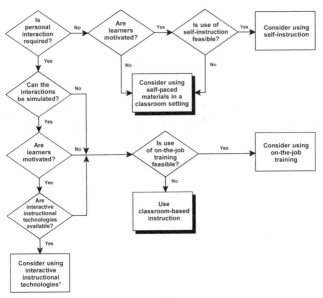

*(e.g., web-based, computer-based, video teletraining, etc.)

Alternative Learning Opportunities

There are many opportunities for learning that take place outside the traditional classroom setting. Some alternative learning opportunities are:

STRATEGY	DESCRIPTION
Critical Incidents	Important events involving successes, mistakes, or experiences in the organization that can be talked about and learned from (for example, case studies based on actual events within the organization)
Participation on Teams	Task forces or working groups can offer opportunities for individual and team learning if the members take time to examine the lessons learned from solving an urgent problem or improving a process *and* communicate those lessons to other groups.
Conferences and Seminars	Participating in professional seminars and conferences can help employees keep up-to-date on current topics.
Team Learning Events	Planned events facilitated by someone outside the organization that provide opportunities for the entire staff to participate.

Work-Based Training Strategies

In a learning organization, managers incorporate training into the work setting. The potential advantages of work-based training include:

Time and Money. It is likely to take less time to train your employees at or near their job location than to send them to a training course. In addition, the total costs of work-based training strategies are often less than those of off-the-job training.

Flexibility. Work-based training strategies can flexibly accommodate the individual needs of your employees and the circumstances in which they work.

Transfer. It may be easier to transfer what has been learned in real job conditions than from simulated conditions used in training courses.

Some of the most common kinds of work-based training strategies include:

- Coaching
- Mentoring
- Structured on-the-job training
- Job performance aids
- Special projects and rotational assignments
- Shadowing assignments

COACHING

Description: Developing and extending the ability and experience of employees by giving them systematically planned and progressively "stretching" tasks to perform, along with continuous appraisal and counseling.

Uses: You should consider using coaching when:

- ✓ There is a need to enhance, improve, or develop skills already being demonstrated

- ✓ Employees have the ability and knowledge, but performance has dropped or is no longer meeting expectations

- ✓ New procedures or technologies are introduced to the work setting

- ✓ Employees have not performed job functions recently

Coaching can also be used with nontraining strategies to provide timely, immediate, and concrete feedback.

Tips:

- ➢ Provide training to individuals who will serve as coaches.

- ➢ Ensure that coaches:

  - Establish an environment conducive to coaching. If possible, provide the coaching in a private setting.
  - Set structured objectives for learning and improvement.
  - Jointly agree on an action plan.
  - Select progressively more difficult assignments.
  - Review progress and provide assistance. Reinforce improvements.
  - Review and confirm new learning.

- ➢ Reinforce coaches.

MENTORING

Description: A process whereby mentors and "mentees" work together to discover and develop the mentee's hidden abilities. Mentoring can be formal or informal, a long-term or short-term investment, a single action or an agreed-upon plan. In a learning organization, anyone can be a mentor: The goal is the empowerment and continuous development of the mentees by developing their abilities and expanding their awareness, insight, and perspective. Mentors can provide exceptional learning experiences for their mentees and can highlight the key ideas and information that make events meaningful.

A good mentoring program provides networking and visibility as well as a good role model.

Essential components of a mentoring program include:

- Identifying and matching mentors/mentees
- Training mentors and preparing mentees
- Monitoring the mentoring process
- Evaluating the program

The mentor must consider:

- What knowledge and wisdom to impart
- What skills need to be taught
- How to best teach the subject matter
- What training schedule should be used

Uses: You should consider using mentoring when:

✓ Orienting new employees

✓ Grooming someone to take over a job or function or to master a craft

✓ There is a need for an employee to have special insight, understanding, or information outside the normal channels or training programs

Tips:

> ➤ Provide training for individuals who will serve as mentors.

> ➤ Match mentoring styles to each mentee's learning style when making assignments.

> ➤ Have both parties state what they hope to gain from the relationship.

> ➤ Ensure that mentors:

>   • Identify mentor and mentee expectations before the relationship begins, and develop a timeframe to complete each goal.

>   • Develop a mutual agreement that specifies specific key indicators that can be measured to ensure that the relationship is working.

>   • Check the key indicators periodically.

> ➤ Deal with problems between mentors and mentees as they arise.

> ➤ Reinforce mentors.

STRUCTURED ON-THE-JOB TRAINING (OJT)

Description: Training that takes place in the normal workplace of the trainee and covers the knowledge, skills, and attitudes appropriate to the correct performance of a task or job. On-the-job training (OJT) may include one-to-one instruction or coaching. The goal of OJT is to master new skills while using them. OJT is not a casual process. You must set up organized programs that include time for practice and coaching during the practice.

Uses: You should consider using OJT when:

✓ The trainee is new to the task or job

✓ It is important to train under actual on-the-job conditions

✓ There is a need to refine knowledge and skills learned through other training methods

✓ New procedures or technologies are introduced

✓ Training time and/or budget is limited

Tips:

➢ Base OJT instruction on a thorough job analysis, which identifies what the job tasks are, how they are to be done, reasons why they are done, and standards for task performance.

➢ Train OJT instructors in one-to-one instructional techniques, coaching skills, and feedback skills. Teach OJT instructors ways to explain how and why to perform tasks. Make sure OJT instructors can demonstrate correct methods for performing a task.

➢ Reward OJT instructors for participating in the program.

➢ Identify expected outcomes of the training and communicate them to the OJT instructors and trainees. Make sure that OJT instructors know how to assess the intended performance levels.

➢ Develop a work progression (simple to complex assignments) that will maximize the trainee's ability to succeed. Adjust the OJT instructor's workload to allow for training time.

➢ Develop checklists to ensure that all objectives have been covered during OJT. These checklists can also be used for documenting performance and providing feedback.

➢ Provide specific feedback on the trainee's and the OJT instructor's performance. Identify areas for further practice and/or learning.

➢ Schedule time and space for the trainees and the OJT instructor to meet privately to exchange feedback.

JOB PERFORMANCE AIDS

Description: Job aids provide employees with guidance on how to perform in the context of their work. Anything that provides on-the-spot, practical guidance can be a job aid. Some examples are checklists, decision aids, procedure manuals, work samples, and algorithms or flowcharts.

Uses: You should consider using job aids when:

✓ The consequences of errors are critical

✓ Procedures are complicated

✓ Tasks are performed infrequently

✓ There is a need to reinforce new skills and knowledge learned through other training methods

✓ New procedures and technologies are introduced

✓ Time and/or budget for training is limited

Tips:

➢ Create job aids by listing tasks of an activity or procedure in the order in which they are supposed to be performed. (You can use a flowchart to identify the tasks.) Keep your task descriptions as short and simple as possible. Use algorithms and flowcharts only for short procedures.

➢ Use "IF–THEN" tables to show the consequences and outcomes/products of each activity or procedure.

➢ Use procedure manuals to provide step-by-step guidelines and examples of how to comply with policies, solve work-related problems, and complete typical work duties.

➢ Provide work samples for employees to save them time and to show them how the work should be done.

➢ Test your job aids before distributing them.

SPECIAL PROJECTS AND ROTATIONAL ASSIGNMENTS

Description:

- **Special projects** are short-term and long-term assignments aimed at a specific outcome over a few months to a year and usually are taken on as an assignment in addition to the current job. Projects are normally carried out with tight deadlines and require individuals to work with unfamiliar people and subject matter.

- **Rotational assignments** are details to another position (preferably outside the current unit) that last one month to one year to help an employee broaden his or her horizons and gain a new or better understanding of how other units operate. Working in a different office with unfamiliar co-workers and new responsibilities can be a challenging learning experience.

Uses: You should consider using special projects and/or rotational assignments as a training strategy to:

✓ Add enrichment to a job

✓ Develop employees in specific areas of knowledge and/or skills

✓ Cross-train employees

✓ Help employees learn new skills

✓ Train people for career advancement

Tips:

➤ Provide training on organization-specific policies, procedures, and/or guidance needed to complete the special project or rotational assignment.

➤ Determine if merit selection procedures must be used for making these assignments. Merit selection procedures must be used to select candidates for programs that:

- Prepare employees for career or occupational changes

- Are part of a promotional program such as upward mobility

- Are required before an employee can be considered for promotion

SHADOWING ASSIGNMENTS

Description: During shadowing assignments, employees "shadow" another employee in a position different from their own for a period of time (usually no less than a day and no more than a week). The "shadowee" is able to observe a daily routine and get a sense of the duties and responsibilities of that job.

Uses: You should consider using shadowing assignments as a training strategy to:

✓ Promote cooperation with employees from other work units.

✓ Educate employees about the needs of internal customers.

✓ Introduce employees to alternative careers or positions within the organization.

Tips:

➤ Establish specific objectives to be derived from the assignment. Develop a list of questions that the shadowing employee must answer based on his or her observation.

➤ Provide background information prior to the assignment to prepare both employees.

➤ Meet with the employee after the assignment to discuss what was learned.

➤ Determine if merit selection procedures must be used for making shadowing assignments.

Summary

You have just reviewed some nontraining and training strategies for enhancing employee performance. The next section, *Managing Training Resources,* provides information about weighing the costs and benefits of the type of training you selected, and provides guidelines for acquiring training resources.

Managing Training Resources

A s most managers know, planning a training program does not end when you select a training strategy. You must first weigh the costs and benefits of the type of training you selected, and then build a business case to secure the necessary resources to deliver the training.

Managing Training Resources

To manage training resources, follow these steps:

Step 1: Weigh costs and benefits.

- Identify potential costs.
- Identify potential benefits.

Step 2: Build a business case.

The following pages explain each of the steps involved in managing training resources.

Step 1: Weigh Costs and Benefits.

Once you have selected a training strategy, you should weigh the potential costs and benefits to make sure that the strategy is cost-effective and meets the business case requirements for investing organizational or unit training resources, if this is necessary. You should be able to answer questions such as:

"What will the organization gain as a result of the training?"

"How much will training cost to obtain that gain?"

IDENTIFY POTENTIAL COSTS.

Prior to making a commitment to provide training, it is important that you fully understand the potential costs. Listed below are potential costs of providing training:

✓ Training attendance costs (salary, travel/per diem, etc.)

✓ Cost of replacing the individual while in training

✓ Training/tuition and material costs

✓ Training development costs (if new training is being developed)

✓ Other training implementation and follow-up costs

IDENTIFY POTENTIAL BENEFITS.

Next, you should balance training costs with the potential benefits to be gained. The chart on the following page summarizes the types of potential benefits that may result from the training.

POTENTIAL BENEFITS	INDICATORS
Increased Outputs *Training may be designed to increase the outputs produced by the employees.*	✓ Number of products produced or services provided ✓ Number of work processes completed ✓ Amount of backlogged work
Time Savings *Training may be aimed at reducing the time it takes to complete job tasks.*	✓ Ratio of productive/nonproductive time ✓ Amount of overtime required ✓ Amount of "break-in" time for new employees ✓ Amount of equipment "down time"
Improved Quality *Training may seek to improve the quality of performance.*	✓ Ration of positive/negative customer feedback ✓ Ration of positive/negative findings from internal audits/ studies ✓ Amount of "rework" required ✓ Percentage of products/services meeting standards ✓ Number of innovative solutions/products developed ✓ Changes in employee morale ✓ Number of grievances and personnel issues
Error Reduction *Training may reduce or prevent errors.*	✓ Number of errors ✓ Number of safety-related complaints ✓ Number of accidents ✓ Number of rule/procedure violations ✓ Number of products/services rejected

DETERMINE IF POTENTIAL BENEFITS JUSTIFY COSTS.

Now that you have estimated the cost of providing training and projected the potential benefits, you should answer the following questions:

"Is the cost of training worth it?"

"If I had to pay for this training out of my own pocket, would I?"

If you answer "no" to these questions, then you need to go back to the drawing board. Remember, you have already determined that the performance gap is worth addressing and that training is needed. Your challenge is to identify a cost-effective way of providing the needed training. Remember to look at alternative training methods and work-based training strategies.

Step 2: Build a Business Case.

You may be asked to build a business case for any training that requires a major investment of organizational resources. A business case presents the rationale used in making decisions about the following areas. Here are some ways to present it:

✓ **Use of inside versus outside training delivery resources**

   "If the organization were to use internal instructors, the productivity costs due to the instructors' absence from their jobs would be 544 hours or 68 days. There is no significant value for the organization to build the internal expertise in this training area because it is not a core organization mission."

✓ **Program length**

   "Based on the anticipated outcomes, a 2–3 hour workshop is warranted."

✓ **Develop or buy the training**

   Lost opportunity costs: *"If the organization were to use internal staff for designing, developing, and pilot testing the program, time/productivity costs would be expensive."*

   Speed requirements: *"Speed is critical to this initiative. There is a mandatory requirement to complete all training within a specified period, and within this fiscal year. If the organization were to handle the training development and delivery, it would take months of additional time and cause major delays during the past fiscal year."*

   Availability: *"High-quality, job-relevant commercial training programs, packages, and materials are available."*

Costs: *"When looking at costs for design, development, delivery, materials, reproduction, distribution, and so on, those costs using organizational internal resources would total over $55,000. Costs using vendor instructors and materials were determined to be $54,600."*

Cost per participant: *"Given the large number of employees being trained (136 sessions), the preferred vendor's costs were extremely low—$7 per employee and $1 per employee for materials."*

✓ **Media and method for training delivery** (e.g., classroom, video, computer-based training, distance or online learning, self-instruction, on-the-job training, job aids, etc.)

  "Given our requirement for small groups of participants, live interaction, and the presence of a skilled instructor, classroom training is the preferred method."

The examples presented above were used to establish a business case for using external training resources.

Summary

Now you are ready to develop or acquire the appropriate training to meet the needs of your unit and deliver the training to your employees. However, there is more to enhancing employee performance than just training. The next section, **Promoting Training Transfer,** will describe how you, as a manager, can ensure that the skills and knowledge acquired during training are transferred to the job.

Promoting Training Transfer

In a learning-organization environment, training **by itself** will not make a difference. You, as a manager, have more influence than the trainers do on the trainees' application of learning on the job.

Promoting Training Transfer

The primary barrier for transfer of training to occur is the absence of reinforcement on the job. The real work begins after the training ends. You will need to coach and motivate trainees after a training event by reminding them of goals and benefits and by recognizing and rewarding their efforts to apply new skills. You will also need to commit the time to make whatever changes are needed to support newly learned skills and behaviors.

You must give consideration to things that happen before, during, and after a training event that contribute to the acquisition of knowledge, skills, and attitudes and to their application in your unit.

The following pages describe what managers should do to help ensure training transfer.

BEFORE TRAINING

Managers need to provide and demonstrate their full support of training. You can involve employees in setting goals for themselves following training, make explicit promises of rewards that can be received if training is successfully transferred, and encourage employees to view training as potentially helpful in their jobs and careers. Managerial support greatly strengthens the likelihood that employees will apply their new learning on the job.

To provide this support before training begins, you should:

✓ **Make sure that selected training programs will meet identified needs.** Examine the training design in detail to confirm and validate that content is based on the training needs.

✓ **Schedule training just before the new skills/knowledge will be used on the job.** Employees should be selected for training when a change in technology occurs, requiring new skills; new job responsibilities are to be assumed because of transfer, promotion, or merger; or the employee's performance has been appraised as requiring substantial and sustained improvements in the near future.

✓ **Discuss the expected performance levels following training.** Openly talk about the potential problems and how they can be prevented, minimized, or overcome.

✓ **Collect baseline performance data and involve trainees in needs assessment procedures.** Training should be designed to solve a present or future problem, overcome a gap or deficiency, or prepare employees for job responsibilities. Managers, trainers, and trainees should participate in identifying training needs. Trainers might become aware of the need for training when a technological conversion is scheduled to take place. Trainees should be involved to help ensure their "buy-in" to the training. Participation by all parties involved in the training will help ensure that important inputs are not overlooked.

✓ **Provide a positive training environment.** In some cases, on-the-job training is appropriate; in other cases, off-site locations are beneficial, particularly when it is important to protect employees from work-related interruptions and distractions. A disruptive or inadequate training environment not only distracts trainees, but can also affect their attitudes toward the value of the training itself.

✓ **Provide the individual work time to complete precourse assignments.** Trainers often develop materials that involve employee participation in advance of training. Monitor the distribution of any precourse materials, have employees complete them by a certain (pretraining) date, provide job release time for their completion, and then discuss them with the employees prior to training. This will help guarantee that all employees have done the advance work required of them, and ensure that all employees are starting at the same place when the training begins.

✓ **Develop a supervisor/trainee contract on how employees will transfer new skills to the job, and the support you will provide.** The contract should specify each party's commitment to maximizing the results of training. The example on the following page shows what type of information this contract may contain.

✓ **Develop assignments so that the individual can apply new skills immediately following the training.** You may want to review background information on each individual to help you make better decisions about impending job assignments and hence strengthen the link between what is to be learned and the opportunity to apply that learning. You will need to assign employees to the kinds of jobs, tasks, or special projects that will not only give them the chance to use what they learned, but actually require them to apply it.

EXAMPLE

EMPLOYEE STATEMENT:

I, _____, would like to participate in the following training program: _____. If selected, I agree to:

a) Attend all sessions.
b) Complete all prework, reading, and other assignments.
c) Actively participate in all training modules, keeping an open mind.
d) Create specific action plans detailing my expected applications of the training content and discuss these with my supervisor.
e) Share highlights of the training with relevant co-workers.

Signature: _____   Date: _____

MANAGER/SUPERVISOR'S STATEMENT:

I, _____, the manager/supervisor of the employee identified above, agree to:

a) Release him/her from sufficient work assignments to allow complete preparation for, and attendance at, all training sessions.
b) Attend and participate in all advance briefing sessions for managers/supervisors.
c) Meet with the employee following training to determine highlights of the session and mutually explore opportunities for applications.
d) Minimize all interruptions to the training.
e) Model the desired behaviors for the employee.
f) Provide encouragement, support, and reinforcement for the new employee behaviors.
g) Provide specific opportunities for the employee to practice the new behaviors and skills.

Signature: _____   Date: _____

DURING TRAINING

✓ **Protect the individual from being interrupted during training.** Work-related interruptions can cause the trainer to become frustrated and even lose the sense of continuity in the training. Employees being trained can become distracted from the learning experience and even question how important their own continuous attendance is. Individuals can miss key facts and principles, group activities, useful illustrations, and relevant materials. Not only will the content not be learned by the individuals as well as it should be, but allowing interruptions can send the message that the training is not really important. Consequently, employees may be less motivated to apply what they have learned back on the job.

✓ **Participate in the training, if required.** Participation will communicate managerial support for the training program, and help convince trainees that what they are learning is important and is endorsed by the organization. Employees observe, listen, and sense what is important when those in positions above them speak and act.

It is important that you model what you want your employees to accept, doing so through direct verbal and behavioral endorsement of the new learning. Some of the ways you can convey the message that learning the new skills and behaviors is important are by:

- Attending training sessions
- Actively participating in open discussions
- Accepting training roles; presenting some of the material
- Declaring and showing support for the use of new knowledge and skills
- Visibly and consistently demonstrating the desired new behaviors

✓ **Monitor attendance and attention to training.** For various reasons, trainees may exhibit inattentiveness, conversational disruptions, napping, or session-skipping. If you participate in all sessions of the training, you can help to forestall or handle dysfunctional behaviors by taking disruptive individuals aside to explore their problems. However, it may not be possible for you to participate fully; therefore, you may just want to systematically drop in for brief periods. This will help alert employees to the fact that you support the training and value the potential learning.

✓ **Plan your assessment of transfer of new skills to the job.** The evaluation process should be designed to provide objective feedback about the use of training-related knowledge and skills. Regular evaluation and feedback will encourage employees to continue working on transfer of new skills.

AFTER TRAINING

✓ **Meet with the individual to discuss the newly acquired skills and knowledge and to identify barriers to using these new skills and knowledge on the job.** Negotiate a "contract" specifying what you will do to remove barriers and to support the use of new skills and knowledge, and what the individual will do to meet new performance expectations (see the contract on page 88 in the *Before Training* section).

✓ **Extend the assignment of the substitute who has been handling the trainee's workload for a brief period of additional time after the trainee returns to work.** The extra support will allow time for the employee to get up to speed and solidify new behavior patterns, and will maximize the opportunity for effective training transfer.

✓ **Conduct practice sessions to help sustain skills used frequently.** "Once trained, always capable" is not generally true. Practice sessions should be carefully designed, complete with performance objectives and tailored methods and materials. They should be briefer than the original training, the primary focus being to provide employees with the opportunity to refresh their memories about the key points, proper procedures, and sequence of steps learned in the initial training program.

✓ **Provide job aids, quick reference guides, and other tools to promote transfer.** However, job aids and other such guides must be used in order to be helpful. Make sure employees are using their job aids: ask probing questions that require the employee to use the job aid, model the behavior by using your own job aid, and/or request the behavior ("Please post the list of steps to take so you won't forget to include them").

✓ **Review performance levels and provide feedback.** Effective reinforcement requires that you administer the reinforcement systematically. Positive reinforcement can be highly effective for cementing a pattern of desirable work behaviors and stimulating their repetition.

✓ **Recognize successful use of new skills.** Determine the preferred forms of recognition and help publicize the successful transfer of skills by commending worthy employees during meetings, by providing individual praise in front of employees' peers, by inviting the communications staff to write feature articles for the newsletter on selected employees, or by nominating successful individuals for "Employee of the Month" (and preferably doing all these things).

Summary

You have now learned a number of strategies to help promote the transfer of skills acquired during training to the job setting. The final section, *Evaluating Training Outcomes,* provides methods for evaluating the effectiveness of the training.

Evaluating Training Outcomes

Evaluating the outcomes of training involves finding out if employees are using the knowledge and skills learned in training once they are back on the job, determining if performance gaps have narrowed as a result of the training, measuring what result the training has had on the organization, and making improvements based on the evaluation information.

Outcome Evaluation Steps

To evaluate outcomes, follow these steps:

Step 1: Determine the value of training.

- Measure training transfer.
- Measure organizational results.

Step 2: Make continuous improvements.

- Troubleshoot any lack of training transfer.
- Use evaluation data in a learning organization.

The following pages explain each of the steps used to evaluate training outcomes.

Step 1: Determine the Value of Training.

Training that is linked to achieving specific performance-based objectives (as earlier identified) should help units within the organization achieve their operational objectives. Managers are under increasing pressure to demonstrate how the training investment related to the accomplishment of corporate goals and operational objectives. To do this, you must first assess if employees are using what they learned in training, and if they are, then measure how the training has affected individual and organizational performance.

MEASURE TRAINING TRANSFER.

Measuring on-the-job application of training (training transfer) involves determining if employees are actually using what they learned and whether or not this is narrowing the performance gap. When measuring transfer, you are trying to determine if a person's behavior has changed as a result of the training and if they are using the knowledge and skills from training on the job.

The following questions can help you determine if training transfer has occurred:

✓ Are the employees using the skills and knowledge they have been taught?

✓ Which new skills or behaviors are being used with the greatest frequency?

✓ Are there any behaviors or skills learned in training that are not being used?

Tips:

➤ Observe actual work performance following training. It is important to discuss the reasons for wanting to observe with the individual. Also, try to be as unobtrusive as possible.

➢ Review work samples or performance records. If you selected a sample of work products, make sure that the sample represents how well the individual has performed throughout the work period.

➢ Interview and/or survey the trainee, supervisor, peers, subordinates, and customers (when appropriate).

➢ Conduct follow-up testing to ensure that employees have retained the skills and knowledge.

MEASURE ORGANIZATIONAL RESULTS.

During the process of selecting training strategies, you should have already estimated the costs of providing training and projected the benefits to be derived. This step involves confirming that those estimates of training costs and benefits were accurate.

As a manager, you may not need to conduct formal return-on-investment studies of training. However, you do need to monitor the expenditure of training resources and be accountable for ensuring that training is cost-effective. You can use the following questions to help you determine if the organization has received benefits from its training investment:

✓ How much has the performance gap narrowed?

✓ Have customer attitudes improved?

✓ Was the money you spent on training worth the improved performance demonstrated by employees?

✓ Is there a direct connection between the investment in training and the accomplishment of specific organizational mission requirements?

✓ If you had to do over again, would you invest in this training again?

Tips: When gathering information about training outcomes, make sure to:

➤ Use whatever means are available to find out if the training has resulted in performance that meets the internal and external customer needs and expectations you identified earlier. Customer service data may exist in the form of:

    ✓ Customer surveys/comment cards
    ✓ Correspondence and telephone logs
    ✓ Media reports
    ✓ Audit reports and studies

➤ Make sure to look at the whole picture in determining the benefits of your training. For example, some gains cannot be measured immediately. It may take more than a few months to realize the benefits from training. Also, there are many non-monetary benefits to training. You should document the intangible benefits along with those benefits that are easy to measure.

Step 2: Make Continuous Improvements.

In a learning organization, the environment is constantly changing, and so are customer needs and requirements. Training effectiveness must be continuously monitored to make continuous improvements and increase customer satisfaction.

TROUBLESHOOT ANY LACK OF TRAINING TRANSFER.

The first step in the continuous improvement process is to make sure training transfer occurred, or to uncover the reasons why training transfer did not occur. Listed below are some common reasons for a lack of training transfer:

The Training:

- ✓ The training content was not relevant to on-the-job requirements or customer needs.
- ✓ The training exercises and simulations were unrealistic.
- ✓ "Bad habits" were developed that now need to be "unlearned."

The Individual:

- ✓ The trainee does not have the ability to perform successfully, even with training.
- ✓ The trainee lacked the motivation needed to learn.

The Work Setting:

- ✓ There was no support provided for changing behavior; managers or other employees may have even discouraged any changes.
- ✓ Too much time has elapsed between the training and the opportunity to use the new knowledge and skills.
- ✓ Appropriate tools and resources were not provided.

USING EVALUATION DATA IN A LEARNING ORGANIZATION

Good data, when properly communicated, can transform organizations. Measuring what the customer wants and determining whether you are providing it will benefit your organization, even before you learn the results. Collecting data forces you to think about how your performance is contributing to achieving the organization's objectives.

Evaluation data tell everyone what they do well and help them measure their own progress and improve their performance on the job. Just collecting evaluation data is not significant. Evaluation data must be used if you are to foster a process of continuous improvement.

Summary

You have now completed the employee development process:

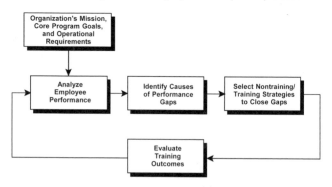

If you find after evaluating the training that performance gaps still exist, you will need to begin the process again by conducting another analysis of employee performance. However, using the employee development process will help ensure competency, productivity, and ultimately, growth within your organization.

Sharon Fisher is Director of Instructional Design for Human Technology, Inc. of McLean, Virginia. Ms. Fisher has designed, developed, and delivered hundreds of instructional interventions for public-sector and private-sector organizations. She specializes in the design of multimedia learning materials in technical and non-technical subject areas.

Ms. Fisher is co-author of *Instructional Systems Design: Volumes I and II, Establishing the Value of Training,* and *Computerized Job Aids for Trainers.*